NEVADA

Past and Present

Greg Roza

rosen publishing's
rosen
central®

New York

Published in 2011 by The Rosen Publishing Group, Inc.
29 East 21st Street, New York, NY 10010

Library of Congress Cataloging-in-Publication Data

Roza, Greg.
Nevada: past and present / Greg Roza. — 1st ed.
    p. cm. — (The United States—past and present)
Includes bibliographical references and index.
ISBN 978-1-4358-9488-4 (library binding)
ISBN 978-1-4358-9515-7 (pbk. book)
ISBN 978-1-4358-9549-2 (6-pack)
1. Nevada—Juvenile literature. I. Title.
F841.3.R69 2010
979.3—dc22

                                                                2010001980

Manufactured in Malaysia

CPSIA Compliance Information: Batch #S10YA: For further information, contact Rosen Publishing, New York, New York, at 1-800-237-9932.

On the cover: Top left: A busy main street in 1903 on the western settlement of Tomapah, Nevada. Top right: Las Vegas, Nevada. Bottom: Two rockets are launched in the Black Rock Desert.

Contents

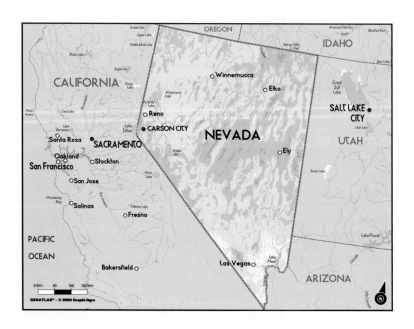

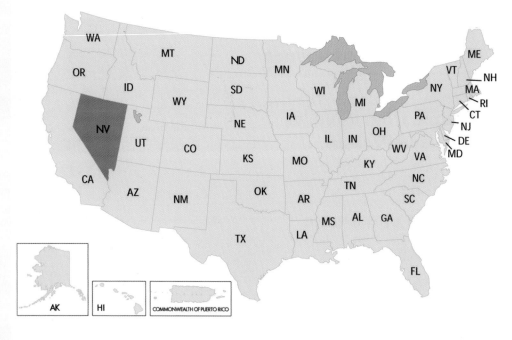

Nevada is geographically the seventh largest state in America. It is situated in the western part of the United States and is bordered by California, Arizona, Utah, Idaho, and Oregon.

Introduction

Nevada is known by many names, and each of them reveals an important aspect of the state. Nevada's official state motto is "All for Our Country." This patriotic motto was written by the Nevada State Senate in 1866, and it has been on the state seal ever since. Nevada became a state in 1864 during the American Civil War. Loyal to the Union, the Nevada Territory was granted statehood and immediately joined in the fight against the Confederacy. The citizens of Nevada took great pride in becoming part of the United States. They showed it in many ways—even in their state motto.

At the same time, and for the same reason, the Battle-Born State quickly became a popular nickname for Nevada. This name was first spoken by Nevada politician Thomas Fitch on July 6, 1864. Referring to the fact that Nevada was joining the Union during the height of the Civil War, Fitch said, "Our state will be battle-born." The nickname stuck; it is even featured on the state flag today.

Nevada is often called the Silver State because of the abundance of silver that has been found there. It is still one of the country's greatest producers of the precious metal. Nevada is also called the Sagebrush State because much of its wild landscape is adorned with this sweet-smelling and hardy bush. It's no wonder that a state as fascinating as Nevada has earned so many diverse names.

Chapter 1

The Geography of NEVADA

Nevada is the seventh largest state by size, measuring about 109,000 square miles (282,309 square kilometers). However, it's thirty-fifth in population with about 2,600,000 people, most of them living in Clark or Washoe counties. That amounts to about twenty-three people per square mile (nine per sq km). The reason for this is because much of Nevada is made up of vast, treeless deserts and tall, rocky peaks.

The Basin and Range Region

Nevada is located almost entirely in a region of the United States called the Great Basin. Water in this area is unable to drain into oceans. Instead, the water collects in "bowls"—low spots in the land—to form small lakes and temporary marshlands.

Many of the lakes in the basin region are ancient bodies of water that used to be much larger. Dried-up lake beds in this area of the world are called playas. Playas have miles and miles of polygon shapes, which form in the damp clay as it dries out and cracks.

Some rivers, such as Nevada's longest, the Humboldt River, flow into areas called sinks. During the rainy season—roughly from December to June when mountain snow melts—water slowly collects

Mount Moriah is the highest peak in the Snake Range and the fifth highest peak in Nevada. It is 12,067 feet (3,678 meters) high.

in shallow lakes and marshes. When the rainy season ends, however, the lakes quickly dry up, leaving flat, dry lakebeds. When these lakebeds are covered with salt sediments, they are called salt flats.

Nevada is home to more than 150 mountain ranges that cross the state. Most of these ranges run in a north-south direction. The Basin and Range Region is a high-altitude basin nestled between the Wasatch Mountains in Utah and the Sierra Nevada Range, which lies mostly in California. The Snake Range is the easternmost in Nevada. The Toquima and Toiyabe ranges run down the center of the state.

Nevada's mountains were formed over the course of millions of years as Earth's crust shifted and pushed the land into the air. These

The Black Rock Desert

The Black Rock Desert is both a geological classroom and a modern playground. At the center of this region is the largest playa in North America—the Black Rock Playa. The desert also has sand dunes, mountains, steppes, sinks, and hot springs. The Black Rock Desert region is about 400 square miles (1,000 sq km) and ranges between 3,500 and 4,000 feet (1,060 and 1,220 meters) above sea level. In the wet season, streams drain from the neighboring mountains into the desert, creating marshes and sinks that sometimes hold up to 5 inches (13 centimeters) of standing water. These areas disappear as the streams dry up, turning the land into a parched desert again.

Millions of years ago, much of Nevada was covered by water. Giant aquatic dinosaurs called ichthyosaurs swam there. Long after the dinosaurs disappeared, this water eventually dried up, leaving the land exposed. Starting in 1928, archaeologists have found more than forty ichthyosaur fossils in the Black Rock Desert. Today, travelers can see several ichthyosaur fossils still embedded in the rock at Berlin-Ichthyosaur State Park.

Between about twenty-five thousand to eleven thousand years ago, an ice age made the climate in Nevada cooler and wetter than it is today. This resulted in the formation of Lake Lahontan. The lake once covered about 8,610 square miles (22,299 sq km), and was about 500 feet (152 m) deep. When this ice age ended, the area became drier. Lake Lahontan dwindled into several smaller lakes. Eventually most of those lakes dried up, resulting in a vast, salt-covered desert.

Today, the Black Rock Desert is home to many unique businesses, pastimes, and attractions. Tourists travel there to see the many geological formations such as salt flats, hot springs, geysers, and Pyramid Lake, which is the largest remaining trace of Lake Lahontan. Some companies mine salts and gypsum there. Others have mined for silver and gold.

forces created numerous ranges, lone hills called buttes, and flat-topped mountains called mesas. Continuing activity in Earth's crust causes earthquakes and geysers. The flat valleys between the ranges are small basins featuring lakes, plains, and marshes.

Old Razorback Mountain stands in the middle of a vast playa in the Black Rock Desert.

The Columbia Plateau Region

The northeastern corner of the state is part of the Columbia Plateau, sometimes called the Columbia Basin. This region extends into Idaho, Oregon, and Washington. Rivers in this area—including the Owyhee River—drain into the Columbia River, which empties into the Pacific Ocean. Geologists call this region a flood basalt plateau. It was formed by enormous volcanic eruptions over the course of millions of years. The constant eruptions spread lava over the land, creating a wide, flat plateau. Over many years, rivers have cut deep canyons in the igneous rock.

The Sierra Nevada Region

The Sierra Nevada Range is a 400-mile (640 km) range that is located mainly in the state of California. A small part of the range crosses over into western Nevada. Many of the range's peaks in Nevada are

Lake Tahoe is a freshwater lake on the border of Nevada and California in the Sierra Nevada Range. Its natural beauty makes it a highly popular destination for tourists.

snowcapped year-round, making it the ideal location for skiing. It is home to Lake Tahoe, which is the second deepest lake in the United States. Lake Tahoe is known for its crystal clear water and its breathtaking natural vistas. Other parts of the range have hot springs and geysers.

The Sierra Nevada Range keeps moisture from the Pacific Ocean from reaching the Nevada interior. However, three of Nevada's largest rivers begin in the Sierra Nevada range: the Carson, Truckee, and Walker rivers. During the spring thaw, these rivers bring water to Nevada's dry landscape.

Climate and Wildlife

Nevada is the driest state in the United States. On average, it receives only 7.5 inches (19 cm) of precipitation a year. Rivers form in the wet season but slow down or dry up soon after. Most of the rivers that flow year-round empty into sinks or ancient lakes. Some valleys get enough water to sustain grassy plains where cattle range.

Although the Basin and Range Region is one of the driest places in the world, it is home to abundant wildlife. Much of the land is covered with sweet-smelling sagebrush and other bushes. Bristlecone pine trees strike twisted poses in the mountains: Some are believed to be more than four thousand years old. The mountainsides have forests containing many types of trees including pine, fir, piñon, and juniper. Valley deserts are home to yuccas, Joshua trees, and many types of cacti. Spring snowmelt allows fields of wildflowers to thrive in many Nevada deserts and grasses to grow in valleys and plains.

Reptiles in Nevada include rattlesnakes, lizards, tortoises, and Gila monsters. Large range animals include bighorn sheep, elk, mule deer, pronghorn antelope, wild horses, and mules. You may also find foxes, rabbits, coyotes, and porcupines. Birds in this region include ducks, geese, falcons, eagles, and owls. Pyramid Lake is home to thousands of white pelicans. Nevada's lakes and streams are home to trout, bass, and perch. Pyramid Lake is home to a rare fish called the cui-ui (KWEE-wee), which is found nowhere else on Earth. Similarly, the Devils Hole pupfish is found only in Devils Hole, a small geothermal pool in the Amargosa Desert.

Chapter 2

THE HISTORY OF NEVADA

When Europeans first arrived in Nevada in the mid-1700s, the native groups included the Northern and Southern Paiute, Shoshone, and Washoe Indians. Life was difficult for these groups, but they were strong and resourceful. Most groups survived by foraging for nuts, seeds, and grasses, and by hunting. Life for the Nevada Indians changed drastically with the arrival of Europeans.

Exploring Nevada

Spain claimed the areas today known as Mexico and the American Southwest in 1776, but they never established any settlements there. The northern section of this rugged area—which they called New Spain—remained largely unexplored until the early 1800s. In time, fur trappers and gold miners took interest in the area.

At the end of the Mexican War for Independence in 1821, New Spain became the property of Mexico. Few attempts had been made to explore the "American desert." A British fur trapper named Peter Skene Ogden led a group into Nevada in 1826, but little came of the trip. Shortly after, American trapper and explorer Jedediah Strong Smith became the first white person to cross and explore the Great Basin and the Sierra Nevada Range.

The Great Basin remained largely untouched by whites for several more decades. This began to change in the 1840s as easterners flooded the area in hopes of finding gold. "Overlanders" began crossing the Great Basin in wagon trains. Many continued on into California and Oregon. Others stayed to mine gold and silver in the desert.

Kit Carson was a trapper, scout, Indian agent, and soldier. Today, he is a well-known legend of the Wild West.

Manifest Destiny

In the 1840s, Americans were gripped by the idea that the United States had the right to claim all the land between the Atlantic and Pacific oceans. This idea was called manifest destiny. U.S. army officer John C. Frémont and his guide Christopher "Kit" Carson explored and mapped the Great Basin and the Sierra Nevada mountain area.

In 1848, the United States won a war with Mexico. As a result, they annexed the area that had once been called New Spain. Manifest destiny had become a reality. At this point, the area that would eventually become Nevada was just one section of a large frontier called the Unorganized Territory.

Mining in Nevada

In 1859, prospectors searching for gold on Mount Davidson discovered a rich deposit of silver ore. The land belonged to a man named Henry Comstock. The deposit became known as the Comstock Lode. Word spread quickly, and prospectors from around the word rushed to the area. Virginia City quickly rose up near the Comstock Lode. At its height, about thirty thousand people lived there. Mining was difficult and dangerous work. Some miners made a fortune, but many others died penniless.

The California Gold Rush and the Nevada mining industry brought many people to Nevada, and the population swelled. Settlements sprang up along the California Trail, where travelers and miners could buy supplies from ambitious businessmen. Many settlements became permanent towns. Other mining towns—such as Virginia City and Rhyolite—went from boomtowns to ghost towns once the silver mines were depleted.

Despite these ups and down, mining continued to play an important role in Nevada's development. Silver deposits were found in areas like Tonopah. Copper ore was discovered near Ely. The United States used silver mined in Nevada to make silver dollars until the 1880s. Gold was discovered near Goldfield in 1902. During World War I, metals such as copper, lead, and zinc were mined to make weapons.

Today, Nevada is the nation's leading producer of gold and the second producer of silver ore. Many other minerals are mined there as well. Improved technology has made finding, mining, and transporting minerals easier, safer, and more productive. The Silver State's rich mining history has become an important source of tourism income. Historic mining towns such as Virginia City are popular tourist attractions. Travelers can learn about the history of mining and even see actual mining materials.

The Utah Territory

One of the first groups to settle in Nevada was the Mormons. Mormon pioneers had begun settling around the Great Salt Lake and other nearby areas in 1847. They petitioned the U.S. government to join the Union as the State of Deseret. Instead, the U.S. government established the Utah Territory in 1850. This territory included the modern state of Utah, most of Nevada, and parts of Colorado and Wyoming.

In 1851, Mormons from Salt Lake City set up a trading post in the Carson Valley.

This photograph from the 1890s shows a silver mining camp at the base of the Sierra Nevada Mountains.

Mormon Station—today called Genoa—became the first permanent, non-Native American settlement in the land today called Nevada. Other Mormon settlements soon followed, including one that would become Las Vegas.

The Road to Statehood

The first transcontinental telegraph, railroads, and the Pony Express all affected the growth of towns in Nevada. As more people moved

Speed skaters practice for the 1960 Winter Olympics in Squaw Valley. Although the Olympics were held in California, they helped draw attention to the natural beauty of nearby Nevada.

west, the United States began organizing the western territories and admitting new states into the Union. In 1861, President James Buchanan signed a bill establishing the Nevada Territory, which separated from the Utah Territory and formed its own territorial government. This was in part a result of arguments between Mormons in Utah and non-Mormons in Nevada. The Nevada Territory sided with the North during the American Civil War. The U.S. government hurried to admit Nevada to the Union to increase its size, strength, and wealth. In 1864, the Battle-Born State became the thirty-sixth state in the Union.

Soon after the war ended, Nevada was rewarded for its loyalty to the United States. In 1866, Nevada's eastern border was moved more than 50 miles (80 km) east, making Nevada bigger and the Utah Territory smaller. Nevada achieved its current proportions in 1867, when a section of the Arizona Territory was added to the state.

Modern Nevada

Nevada went through several silver and gold rushes after 1867, but it remained one of the least populated states in the Union. The population began to grow steadily in 1931 when construction on the Hoover Dam began.

Starting in 1951, the U.S. military conducted nuclear testing in the deserts of Nevada; these tests had long been the subject of controversy. The 1960 Winter Olympics, held in Squaw Valley, California, near Lake Tahoe, brought the surrounding areas of Nevada into the spotlight. Today, Nevada holds many attractions for visitors from all over the world—geological fascinations, historic locations, and dazzling modern sites. It's all in Nevada.

THE GOVERNMENT OF NEVADA

Over the years, many governments have ruled Nevada. Native American, Spanish, and Mexican governments controlled the area before it became a U.S. territory. After the United States gained control of the American Southwest, Nevada was governed by temporary governments of the New Mexico, Utah, Arizona, and Nevada territories.

The Nevada State Constitution was created in Carson City on July 4, 1864. It became official on October 31, 1864, when President Abraham Lincoln admitted Nevada into the Union. Nevada's constitution outlines the duties of the state government and defines state laws. Just like the U.S. federal government, the Nevada state government is made up of three separate but equal parts, or branches. Each branch has powers over the other two, creating a system of checks and balances.

Legislative Branch

The Nevada State Legislature creates state laws. It is a bicameral governmental body, meaning it is made up of two houses: the state senate and the state assembly. Both houses are made up of elected officials who represent the citizens of Nevada.

Nevada state legislators and their families gather in the Assembly Chambers in Carson City on February 2, 2009.

The state senate has twenty-one members, each of whom is elected to a four-year term. The state assembly is made up of forty-two members. Each member of the assembly is elected to a two-year term. Legislative sessions begin in January of odd-numbered years. Many legislators serve on boards and committees between sessions.

During a legislative session, lawmakers introduce bills. A committee is formed in one of the houses to discuss a bill. The committee may decide that the bill is not good for the state, or they may also amend, or change, the bill before approving it. If the committee decides it is a good idea, the entire house or assembly votes on it. When a bill passes this vote, it is sent to the other house for another

Carson City

In 1851, ranchers in the Eagle Valley established the Eagle Station trading post. In 1858, a pioneer and businessman named Abe Curry surveyed the land and plotted a town site.

The settlement was renamed Carson City after Christopher "Kit" Carson, the frontiersman and scout who had helped John C. Frémont explore the area. When the Comstock Lode was discovered nearby in 1859, Carson City became an important business and transportation hub.

Carson City became the territorial capital in 1861. It also became the capital of Ormsby County. Abe Curry leased the Warm Springs Hotel to the new legislature to use as a meeting place. It was also used as a prison. Nevada gained statehood in 1864, and Carson City became the state capital. The U.S. Mint was completed in Carson City in 1869. The Nevada State Capitol building, which is still used today, was completed in 1870.

In the following years, the Comstock Lode and the timber industry kept Carson City growing. However, the Comstock Lode stopped producing silver in the 1880s. Soon after, newer railroad lines were constructed that bypassed Carson City. The population dropped to about 1,800 people—about a quarter of what it had once been. The capital became a tiny, quiet town.

It wasn't until the 1960s that the population of Carson City reached the numbers it had during the height of the Comstock Lode. In 1969, the Ormsby County and Carson City governments were consolidated into a single municipal body, and Ormsby County was renamed Carson City County. Today, many of the city's original buildings are museums.

Over the years, the original capitol building has been remodeled and expanded. It is part of the capitol complex along with the legislative building, the supreme court, and the state library and archives. Altogether, the city covers 146 square miles (378 sq km). Once one of the smallest and most rustic state capitals in the United States, Carson City is now one of the largest and most beautiful.

vote. If it passes the vote in both houses, the bill is sent to the governor. The governor can either sign the bill into law or veto (decline) it. However, the legislature can overrule a veto with a two-thirds majority vote.

Executive Branch

The executive branch enforces the laws created by the legislature. It also makes suggestions to the legislature regarding state issues, such as the use of state funds.

The Nevada governor's mansion in Carson City, shown here, was completed in 1909.

Executive officials are elected by the citizens of Nevada. They serve four-year terms and can be reelected just once.

The head of the executive branch is called the governor. This official enforces state laws. The next highest official is the lieutenant governor. He or she takes over if the governor is unable to do his or her job. The lieutenant governor is also leader of the state senate. There are four other elected executive officials. The attorney general is the chief law enforcement officer. The secretary of state monitors state elections. The controller and treasurer manage state funds.

All executive officers oversee the actions of various state departments and agencies. The governor appoints members to departments and agencies. These include groups such as the departments of

The Nevada State Supreme Court has heard cases in four different buildings. This is the current supreme court building, which was completed in 1992.

tourism and transportation, and the Nevada Commission on Economic Development.

Judicial Branch

Nevada's judicial branch is made up of many courts and judges. This branch interprets state laws and determines the punishment for those who break them. It settles public and private disputes by applying the laws of the state constitution.

The highest court in Nevada is the state supreme court. Nevada's citizens elect seven supreme court justices to six-year terms. The justices choose one of the seven to be the chief justice for a two-year term. The supreme court is a court of appeals. This means that it reviews cases tried in lower courts to make sure the decisions follow the law of the state constitution. The supreme court also determines the legality of laws created by the state legislature.

Beneath the supreme court are district courts, justice of the peace courts, and city or municipal courts. District courts hear family, criminal, civil, and juvenile cases. Justice of the peace courts hear cases about minor crimes. City or municipal courts deal with smaller, local cases, such as traffic violations.

Government at the Local Level

In addition to the state government, Nevada has seventeen county governments led by a board of commissioners. Counties elect district attorneys, sheriffs, and other officials. Most cities in Nevada are governed by a mayor and a city council. There are also many tribal governments in Nevada.

Voters in Nevada can use the initiative process to create laws. They do this by signing a petition. If enough people sign the petition, the proposed law is placed on the next general election ballot. If it passes the vote, it must be approved a second time during the next general election. The initiative process ensures that Nevada citizens live in a truly democratic environment.

Chapter 4

THE ECONOMY OF NEVADA

More than half of those employed in Nevada work in the service industry. These workers do things for other people, and they include doctors, lawyers, cooks, teachers, construction workers, librarians, real estate agents, and many others. Manufacturers and warehouses are two more important employers in the state.

Nevada's most important service industry is tourism. Nevada casinos and resorts make so much money that Nevada citizens don't have to pay personal income tax. In addition, Nevada does not have a corporate income tax, which encourages the growth of businesses and industries.

Tourism

Unlike most states, which get most of their income from the service industry and manufacturing, Nevada's greatest source of income is tourism. More than 50 percent of the tax dollars collected by the Nevada government come from services related to the tourism industry. Resort areas and casinos are the greatest source of tourist dollars. Each year, more than fifty million tourists travel to Nevada to enjoy various activities such as legalized gambling, theatrical shows, historic attractions, mountain resorts, and college sporting events.

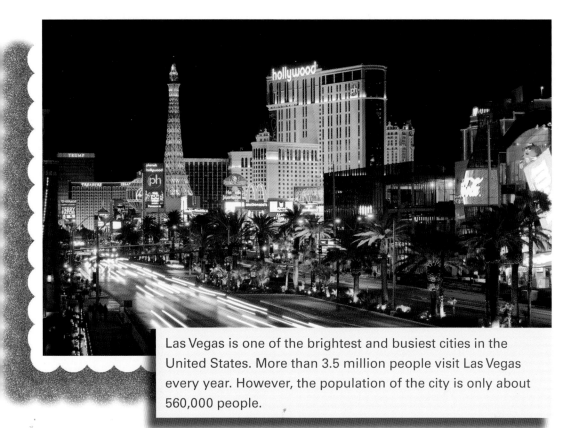

Las Vegas is one of the brightest and busiest cities in the United States. More than 3.5 million people visit Las Vegas every year. However, the population of the city is only about 560,000 people.

Las Vegas and Reno

In 1931, Nevada became the first state to legalize casino gambling. Las Vegas quickly grew with the construction of casinos. In the 1940s, the population grew from about 8,400 people to more than 24,000. Many of these people worked in Las Vegas's tourism-related service industries. Flashy, modern casinos became hot spots for travelers from all over the country. Not only did people travel there to play games, but they also went there to see famous comedians, musicians, actors, and dancers. Popular performers, such as Sammy Davis Jr. and Frank Sinatra, entertained people night after night.

The Hoover Dam and Nevada's Economy

The Great Depression was a time of enormous hardship for American citizens. Many people throughout the country were unemployed and struggled to survive. A massive federal construction project on the border between Nevada and Arizona provided thousands of men with jobs. The Hoover Dam, originally called the Boulder Dam, is 30 miles (48 km) southeast of Las Vegas. When it was completed in 1936, it was the biggest dam in the world. The Hoover Dam helped shape the economy of Nevada.

Construction began on the dam in 1931. The U.S. government planned the project to help control flooding in the region and to provide water for farms in the American Southwest. The project required a workforce of more than twenty-one thousand workers. Men from all over the country migrated to the area with their families in hopes of landing a job. A report from the 1930s shows that 5,522 Nevadans worked on the dam. This number was higher than any other state.

Far more workers arrived than could be hired for the job. However, the result was similar to the migration that occurred during the gold and silver rushes. Nevada's population swelled. After the dam was finished, many families chose to settle in Nevada. Las Vegas grew from a small town into a large city, thanks in part to the mammoth construction project. The electricity created by hydroelectric generators at the dam also helped Nevada grow.

Today, the Hoover Dam continues to have an impact on Nevada's economy. Agriculture is possible in the desert region today, thanks to Lake Mead, the massive reservoir created by the dam. Since its completion, aqueducts and pumping stations have been built to bring water to farms in southern Nevada. In addition, Lake Mead—the largest reservoir in the United States—is a popular tourist destination. Leisure activities include boating, fishing, swimming, camping, and cycling.

Today, Las Vegas continues to reinvent itself. Casinos are no longer the only attraction. Las Vegas also features amusement parks, theaters, concerts, magic shows, and much more. These attractions have made Las Vegas the perfect place for kids and adults alike, while allowing Nevada's largest city to grow and prosper.

Reno—the Biggest Little City in the World—features many of the same types of attractions as Las Vegas. Each year, hundreds of people flock to Reno for the Great Reno Balloon Race. Reno is also a popular destination for travelers on their way to some of Nevada's greatest scenic treasures.

A skier enjoys the view of Lake Tahoe from a nearby slope.

Resort Areas

Some travelers steer clear of the neon lights and flashy shows in favor of quieter and more scenic locations. Just 26 miles (42 km) south of Reno is Nevada's capital, Carson City, a city rich in history and culture. Nearby is the beautiful Lake Tahoe, the largest alpine lake in North America. Lake Tahoe is surrounded by many tourist attractions. The lake is the second deepest in the United States and is a popular location for scuba divers. Winter activities are popular,

The Hoover Dam contains 3.25 million cubic yards (2.48 million cubic meters) of concrete. The project was finished two years ahead of schedule, in 1935.

including skiing, snowshoeing, sledding, and snowmobile riding. Other leisure activities include hiking, bicycling, boating, swimming, and fishing.

Some popular tourist destinations in Nevada include Laughlin (another great place for hot air balloon enthusiasts), the Hoover Dam, gold mines, and ghost towns.

Mining

An industry vital to the growth of Nevada, mining is still important to the state. About three-quarters of the gold mined in the United States comes from Nevada mines. The state is second to Alaska in the production of silver. Other metals mined in Nevada include copper, magnesium, and mercury. Nevada is the country's top producer of barite, a mineral used to make the materials needed for oil wells. Minerals used in the construction industries that are mined in Nevada include gypsum, clay, sand, limestone, salt, and gravel. Gemstones, such as turquoise and opals, are also mined there.

Agriculture

Most of Nevada's farms are ranches for cattle and sheep. The average ranch in Nevada is about 2,000 acres (809 hectares), and many ranchers rent land from the U.S. government. Beef cattle is the state's biggest farm product. Other important livestock include sheep, horses, dairy cattle, and pigs.

The state's leading crop is alfalfa, which is used as feed for cattle. Other crops include barley, garlic, mint, onions, potatoes, and wheat. The lack of water in Nevada has always made agriculture difficult. Most farming occurs in river valleys with the aid of irrigation.

Chapter 5

PEOPLE FROM NEVADA:
PAST AND PRESENT

The names of many entertainers have become synonymous with Nevada, particularly those who have become famous by performing in Las Vegas. These include singers like Frank Sinatra and Wayne Newton, musicians like Liberace, and magicians like Siegfried and Roy. The writer Samuel Clemens assumed his more famous name—Mark Twain—while working as a reporter in Virginia City. Many famous people have risen to prominence in Nevada.

Nevada has also been the home of many notable celebrities and historic figures. These include politicians, Native Americans, athletes, and others. Read on to learn more about famous Nevadans.

Eva Bertrand Adams (1908–1991) Eva Bertrand Adams was born in Wonder, Nevada, in 1908. She spent much of her childhood in Reno. After graduating from high school, she received college degrees from the University of Nevada and Columbia University in New York City. She taught English at the University of Nevada before becoming an administrative assistant to Nevada Senator Pat McCarran in 1940. During this time she also earned a law degree.

In 1961, President John F. Kennedy asked her to become director of the U.S. Mint. She held this position from

1961 to 1969. Adams is credited with modernizing the mint and increasing the production of coins. She approved and supervised the construction of a new mint in Philadelphia, Pennsylvania.

Andre Agassi (1970–) Andre Agassi was born in Las Vegas on April 29, 1970. Andre became interested in tennis at a very early age. He turned pro when he was just sixteen. During his tennis career, Agassi won 689 singles matches, including eight Grand Slam singles competitions: four Australian Opens, two U.S. Opens, one French Open, and one Wimbledon. Agassi won a gold medal at the 1996 Olympic Games.

Agassi retired from professional tennis in 2006. Since then, he has devoted much of his time to charity. In 1994, he founded the Andre Agassi Foundation, which gives assistance to children from low-income families in southern Nevada. Today, he is involved in several charitable projects to help at-risk kids reach their full potential.

Kurt Busch (1978–) and Kyle Busch (1985–) Two of NASCAR's top drivers are brothers from Las Vegas. Kurt Busch was born on August 4, 1978, and his brother Kyle was born on May 2, 1985. The brothers' father and grand-father were also racecar drivers. They learned about racing and cars by watching their father at the racetrack and in the garage.

Kurt won the NASCAR Sprint Cup in 2004. That year, he had twenty-one top-ten finishes and twelve top-five finishes. Kyle won the Sprint Cup Rookie of the Year award in 2005.

James E. Casey (1888–1983) Born in Pick Handle Gulch, Nevada, in 1888, James E. Casey founded one of the most successful companies of the twentieth century—United Parcel Shipping, or UPS. In 1907, Casey borrowed $100 from a friend to start a messenger service in Seattle, Washington. Initially, Casey used foot messengers and two bicycles to deliver packages and letters. In 1913, UPS purchased its first delivery car, and the business began to grow quickly. Eventually the company branched out to the rest of the country.

The Busch brothers talk before a race at Las Vegas Motor Speedway on March 9, 2007.

Casey prided himself on offering cheap rates and dependable service. He also treated his employees very well. Thanks to Casey's business wisdom, UPS is one of the biggest package services in the world today.

Edith Head (1897–1981) World-renowned fashion designer Edith Head lived in the tiny town of Searchlight as a child, where her father was a mining engineer. After teaching high school French, Head became a costume designer in Hollywood. She made clothes for many famous actors. Head won eight Academy Awards, more than any other woman.

Jack Kramer (1921–2009) Another Nevada tennis legend, Jack Kramer, was born in Las Vegas on August 1, 1921. When he was just eighteen, Kramer became the youngest person to play in the Davis Cup title round. Kramer won thirteen U.S. singles and doubles titles during his career. He was inducted into the Tennis Hall of Fame in 1968.

After Kramer retired, he became an energetic tennis promoter. He was the first executive director for the Association of Tennis Professionals (ATP), which was founded in 1972. Kramer was also a tennis announcer for several years. Today, Kramer is remembered as one of the greatest athletes to play the game.

Greg LeMond (1961–) Greg LeMond was born in California, and he grew up in Washoe Valley, Nevada. In 1986, LeMond became the first American to win the Tour de France. Shortly after his victory, LeMond was accidentally shot while hunting with a relative. He nearly died, and everyone thought his cycling career was over.

LeMond's rehabilitation was very difficult. Thanks to several cycling innovations—including wind-tunnel testing, lightweight frames, and heart rate monitors—LeMond returned to racing form. Against all odds, LeMond won the

Native Americans in Nevada

Native Americans first arrived in Nevada about twelve thousand years ago. Early Native Americans left behind stone tools, wooden carvings, and other relics. Archaeologists have found cave drawings called petroglyphs in Valley of Fire State Park near Las Vegas and Grimes Point near Fallon.

As Lake Lahontan dried up, life changed for Native Americans in Nevada. Farming became difficult, so they relied more on hunting and foraging. Most groups roamed the wilderness instead of settling in one area. In time, four main groups developed: the Washoe, Shoshone, Northern Paiute, and Southern Paiute.

In 1843, explorer John C. Frémont hired Northern Paiute Chief Truckee as a guide. Today, the Truckee River bears his name. Another Northern Paiute chief, Winnemucca, advocated peace between Indians and whites. Winnemucca's daughter Thocmetony (later Sarah Winnemucca) learned English. She became an interpreter and scout for the U.S. Army. In 1883, she wrote *Life Among the Paiutes*, making her the first Indian woman to publish a book in English. Another Northern Paiute, Wovoka or Jack Wilson, had a vision of peace. He taught his people the Ghost Dance to help his vision come true. Wovoka's teachings spread to other Indian groups across the Great Plains.

Today, dozens of federally recognized Indian groups live on tribally owned lands in Nevada called reservations. Some Native Americans, such as Southern Paiute Alfreda Mitre, have helped their people modernize their communities, allowing them to compete economically with non-Native businesses.

This portrait of Winnemucca was taken around 1880.

1989 Tour de France and the 1989 World Cycling Championship. He won a third Tour de France in 1990 before retiring.

Pat Nixon (1912–1993) Former First Lady Pat Nixon—wife of President Richard Nixon—was born in 1912 in Ely, Nevada. During World War II, Nixon worked as an economist for the U.S. government. She also worked for the Red Cross and raised two daughters. When Richard Nixon became president in 1968, Pat became an advocate for volunteerism and community service. She was also a member of several important presidential committees, including the Committee on Employment of the Handicapped and the Right to Read program. During her time as first lady, Nixon helped collect about six hundred antiques and works of art for the White House art collection. Today, she is remembered for her worldwide efforts to help the "common man."

Harry Reid (1939–) Harry Reid was born in Searchlight, Nevada, on December 2, 1939. As a boy, Reid helped his father in nearby gold mines. Reid attended college in Utah and then earned a law degree from George Washington University in Washington, D.C.

Reid became the city attorney of Henderson, Nevada. In 1968, he was elected to the Nevada State Assembly. Two years later, he became the youngest lieutenant governor in Nevada history. In 1977, he became the chairman of the Nevada Gaming Commission. Reid served two terms in the U.S. House of Representatives beginning in 1983. He was first

Harry Reid has been elected to the Senate four times: in 1986, 1992, 1998, and 2004. He has also served as the chairman of several important committees and subcommittees.

elected to the U.S. Senate in 1986, and he has been a Nevada senator ever since. Reid, a Democrat, is well-known for his leadership skills and has been the majority leader since 2006.

Yonema Tomiyasu (1882–1969) Yonema Tomiyasu was one of the first Japanese Americans to settle in southern Nevada. Tomiyasu had been living in California, but he moved to Nevada because, at the time, Asian Americans were not allowed to own ranches there. Farming was difficult in southern Nevada. However, Tomiyasu experimented with many different types of crops to make money. He developed farm techniques that allowed him to grow food in the desert. He met with great success in the 1930s when he supplied Hoover Dam workers with food. Prior to Tomiyasu's innovative agricultural techniques, most fruits and vegetables had to be shipped to Las Vegas from hundreds of miles away. His tomatoes, asparagus, watermelons, and cantaloupe were very popular with the workers and with locals as well.

Timeline

12,000 years ago Paleo-Indians first arrive in the area today known as Nevada.

1776 Spain claims the area today known as Mexico and the American Southwest.

1826 Jedediah Strong Smith becomes the first white person to cross the Great Basin and Sierra Nevada mountains.

1844 Northern Paiute Truckee guides a wagon train from Humboldt Sink to the river that today bears his name.

1851 Mormons from Salt Lake City set up the trading post Mormon Station. Ranchers set up the Eagle Station trading post.

1859 The Comstock Lode is discovered.

1861 President James Buchanan signs a bill establishing the Nevada Territory. Carson City becomes the territorial capital.

1864 Nevada becomes the thirty-sixth state.

1883 Sarah Winnemucca becomes the first Native American woman to publish a book in English.

1928 Archaeologists begin finding ichthyosaur fossils in the Black Rock Desert.

1931 Construction on the Hoover Dam begins. Nevada becomes the first state to legalize casino gambling.

1939 Harry Reid is born in Searchlight, Nevada.

1951 The U.S. military begins conducting nuclear tests in the deserts of Nevada.

1969 The Ormsby County and Carson City governments are consolidated into a single municipal body, and Ormsby County is renamed Carson City County.

1997 British air force pilot Andy Green becomes the first person to drive a jet-propelled car faster than the speed of sound in the Black Rock Desert.

2008 The area around Reno experiences more than one thousand earthquakes—mostly minor—over the course of several months, the strongest occurring on April 25; the Nevada Bureau of Land Management records its one millionth mining claim.

State bird:	Mountain bluebird
State flower:	Sagebrush
State motto:	"All for Our Country"
State capital:	Carson City
State trees:	Bristlecone pine and the single-leaf piñon
Statehood date and number:	October 31, 1864; thirty-sixth state
State nicknames:	The Battle-Born State, the Silver State, the Sagebrush State
Total area:	110,567 square miles (286,367 sq km); seventh largest state
Population:	2.6 million
Highest elevation:	Boundary Peak, 13,140 feet (4,005 m) above sea level
Lowest elevation:	Colorado River, 479 feet (146 m) above sea level
Major rivers:	Colorado River, Columbia River, Humboldt River

State flag

State seal

Major lakes:	Pyramid Lake, Lake Mead, Lake Tahoe
Hottest recorded temperature:	125 degrees Fahrenheit (52 degrees Celsius) at Laughlin on June 29, 1994
Coldest recorded temperature:	–50°F (–46°C) at San Jacinto on January 8, 1937
Origin of state name:	Spanish for "snow-covered"
Chief agricultural products:	Cattle, alfalfa, barley, garlic, mint, onions, potatoes, wheat
Major industries:	Tourism, manufacturing, mining

Mountain bluebird

Sagebrush

GLOSSARY

alfalfa A plant in the pea family used to feed cattle.

alpine A region on high mountains above the timberline, or the line past which trees can't grow.

annex To take over a territory.

archaeologist Someone who studies ancient cultures by examining their material remains.

barite A yellowish-white mineral used in the oil-drilling industry.

basalt A hard, black volcanic rock.

basin A broad area of land where rain and snowmelt drain into a body of water.

bicameral Made up of two government bodies.

casino A place where gambling takes place.

economist An expert in the field of economics.

geothermal Relating to the heat in the interior of Earth.

geyser A hot water spring that forces a jet of water and steam into the air at regular intervals.

gypsum A white mineral used in the production of cement, plaster, and fertilizers.

hydroelectric Relating to the generation of electricity by means of water pressure.

ice age A period in Earth's history when temperatures fell worldwide and areas of Earth's surface were covered with glaciers.

igneous rock Rock formed from hardened lava or magma.

Mormon A member of the Church of Jesus Christ of Latter-day Saints.

municipal Relating to an area that has its own government.

petroglyph A prehistoric drawing done on rock.

playa The lower region of an inland basin that periodically becomes covered with shallow water.

prospector Someone who explores an area in search of gold, silver, or other valuable minerals.

reservoir A large natural or artificial lake used for collecting and storing water for human use.

scuba diving The activity of swimming underwater using an oxygen tank and breathing mask.

steppe A mostly treeless, dry plain covered with grasses.

Berlin-Ichthyosaur State Park

HC 61 Box 61200

Austin, NV 89310

(775) 964-2440

Web site: http://www.parks.nv.gov/bi.htm

Established in 1957, this state park protects and displays ichthyosaur fossils. The park also preserves the mining town of Berlin and the Diana Mine.

Friends of Black Rock/High Rock

Box 224, 380 Main Street

Gerlach, NV 89412

(775) 557-2900

Web site: http://www.blackrockdesert.org

This organization helps manage the resources of the Black Rock Desert region and educates the public regarding the importance of preserving the desert's natural beauty.

Nevada Bureau of Mines and Geology (NBMG)

Mail Stop 178

University of Nevada

Reno, NV 89557-0178

(775) 784-6691

Web site: http://www.nbmg.unr.edu

The bureau is a research and public service division of the University of Nevada. NBMG scientists carry out research and publish reports on minerals, geology, environmental resources, and geologic mapping.

Nevada Commission on Tourism

401 North Carson Street

Carson City, NV 89701

(800) NEVADA-8 [638-2328]

Web site: http://travelnevada.com

This is the state department responsible for promoting and marketing tourism in Nevada.

Nevada Department of Cultural Affairs

716 North Carson Street, Suite B

Carson City, NV 89701

(775) 687-8393

Web site: http://nevadaculture.org

This is the state department responsible for promoting state cultural activities and maintaining state cultural resources.

Web Sites

Due to the changing nature of Internet links, Rosen Publishing has developed an online list of Web sites related to the subject of this book. This site is updated regularly. Please use this link to access the list:

http://www.rosenlinks.com/uspp/nvpp

Aldridge, Rebecca. *The Hoover Dam*. New York, NY: Chelsea House Publications, 2009.

Bly, Stephen. *Dangerous Ride Across Humboldt Flats*. Wheaton, IL: Crossway Books, 2003.

Brown, Jonathan A. *Nevada*. New York, NY: Gareth Stevens Publishing, 2005.

Burke, Rick. *Kit Carson*. Chicago, IL: Heinemann Library, 2003.

Calvert, Patricia. *Kit Carson: He Led the Way*. New York, NY: Benchmark Books, 2006.

Ditchfield, Christin. *The Shoshone*. Edina, MN: Children's Press, 2004.

Doherty, Craig A. *Great Basin Indians*. New York, NY: Chelsea House Publications, 2010.

Gibson, Karen B. *The Great Basin Indians: Daily Life in the 1700s*. Mankato, MN: Capstone Press, 2005.

Gray, Susan Heinrichs. *Ichthyosaurs*. Mankato, MN: Child's World, 2005.

Gray-Kanatiiosh, Barbara A. *Paiute*. Edina, MN: Abdo Publishing Company, 2007.

Hana, John. *Nevada*. Milwaukee, WI: World Almanac Library, 2003.

Heinrichs, Ann. *Nevada*. New York, NY: Children's Press, 2008.

Hicks, Terry Allen. *Nevada*. New York, NY: Marshall Cavendish Benchmark, 2005.

Landau, Elaine. *The Pony Express*. New York, NY: Children's Press, 2006.

Mann, Elizabeth. *The Hoover Dam: The Story of Hard Times, Tough People, and the Taming of a Wild River*. New York, NY: Mikaya Press, 2006.

Roza, Greg. *The Hoover Dam: Applying Problem-Solving Strategies*. New York, NY: Rosen Publishing Group, 2005.

Souza, D. M. *John C. Frémont*. New York, NY: Scholastic, 2004.

Williams, Suzanne M. *Nevada*. New York, NY: Children's Press, 2003.

Zollman, Pam. *Lake Tahoe*. Danbury, CT: Children's Press, 2006.

BIBLIOGRAPHY

Bilbo, Mike, and Barbara Bilbo. "The Black Rock Desert Landscape." Friends of Black Rock/High Rock, January 3, 2008. Retrieved September 24, 2009 (http://blackrock desert.org/friends/black-rock-desert-landscape).

Biography Channel. "Edith Head." Retrieved October 18, 2009 (http://www.thebiography channel.co.uk/biography_story/433:251/1/Edith_Head.htm).

Bureau of Reclamation. "Hoover Dam: Essays." U.S. Department of the Interior, September 10, 2004. Retrieved October 17, 2009 (http://www.usbr.gov/lc/hoover dam/History/essays.html).

Bureau of Reclamation. "Hoover Dam Workforce." U.S. Department of the Interior, September 10, 2004. Retrieved October 17, 2009 (http://www.usbr.gov/lc/hoover dam/History/essays/workforc.html).

Carson City. "About Carson City: History." June 12, 2006. Retrieved October 6, 2009 (http://www.carson-city.nv.us/index.aspx?page=140).

Erickson, Robert. "Nevada State Government: An Overview." Online Nevada Encyclopedia, February 7, 2008. Retrieved October 6, 2009 (http://www.online nevada.org/nevada_state_government:_an_overview).

Greg LeMond. "About Greg." Retrieved October 18, 2009 (http://www.greglemond.com/aboutgreg.html).

Hana, John. *Nevada*. Milwaukee, WI: World Almanac Library, 2003.

Hattori, Eugene. "Ice Age Nevada and Lake Lahontan." Online Nevada Encyclopedia, April 30, 2007. Retrieved September 24, 2009 (http://www.onlinenevada.org/ice_age_nevada_and_lake_lahontan).

Heinrichs, Ann. *Nevada*. New York, NY: Children's Press, 2008.

Hicks, Terry Allen. *Nevada*. New York, NY: Marshall Cavendish Benchmark, 2005.

Hopkins, A. D. "Alfreda Mitre." *Las Vegas Review-Journal*. Retrieved October 18, 2009 (http://www.1st100.com/part3/mitre.html).

HowStuffWorks. "Geography of Nevada." March 30, 2008. Retrieved October 7, 2009 (http://geography.howstuffworks.com/united-states/geography-of-nevada1.htm).

International Tennis Hall of Fame. "Jack Albert Kramer." Retrieved October 18, 2009 (http://www.tennisfame.com/famer.aspx?pgID=867&hof_id=178).

Latimore, Carey. "Andre Agassi." The Biography Channel. Retrieved October 18, 2009 (http://www.thebiographychannel.co.uk/biography_story/1441:1635/1/Andre_Agassi.htm).

National First Ladies Library. "First Lady Biography: Pat Nixon." Retrieved October 18, 2009 (http://www.firstladies.org/biographies/firstladies.aspx?biography = 38).

Nevada History. "Native Americans in Early Nevada." Retrieved October 18, 2009 (http://nevada-history.org/indians.html).

Nevada State Library and Archives. "Frequently Asked Questions of Nevada Facts." Retrieved October 7, 2009 (http://nevadaculture.org/nsla/index.php?option = com_content&task = view&id = 1141&Itemid = 410#motto).

Oakley, Nancy. "Eva Bertram Adams." Nevada Women's History Project. University of Nevada, Reno. Retrieved October 18, 2009 (http://www.unr.edu/nwhp/bios/women/adams.htm).

Parker, Renee, and Steve George, eds. *Political History of Nevada*. Carson City, NV: State Printing Office, 2006.

Rocha, Guy. "Myth #102: Battle Born and Legal." Nevada State Library and Archives. Retrieved October 7, 2009 (http://nevadaculture.org/nsla/index.php?option = com_content&task = view&id = 783&Itemid = 95).

Shown, James. "The Rise and Fall of Native Americans in Early Nevada History." Nevada History. Retrieved September 28, 2009 (http://nevada-history.org/indians.html).

United Parcel Service. "Company History." Retrieved October 18, 2009 (http://www.ups.com/content/us/en/about/history/index.html).

U.S. Senator for Nevada. "About Harry Reid." Retrieved October 18, 2009 (http://reid.senate.gov/about/index.cfm).

Whitely, Joan. "Bill Tomiyasu." *Las Vegas Review-Journal*. Retrieved October 18, 2009 (http://www.1st100.com/part1/tomiyasu.html).

Williams, Suzanne M. *Nevada*. New York, NY: Children's Press, 2003.

INDEX

About the Author

Greg Roza has been creating educational materials for schools and libraries for ten years. He has a master's degree from SUNY Fredonia. Roza lives in Hamburg, New York, with his wife, Abigail, and their three children—Autumn, Lincoln, and Daisy. He has traveled to locations all over the United States, including Las Vegas, Reno, Pyramid Lake, and the Hoover Dam.

Photo Credits

Cover (top left) American Stock/Hulton Archive/Getty Images; cover (top right) pp. 3, 6, 10, 12, 18, 24, 25, 30, 38 Shutterstock.com; cover (bottom), p. 9 http://en.wikipedia.org/wiki/Black_Rock_Desert; p. 4 © GeoAtlas; p. 7 http://en.wikipedia.org/wiki/File:MtMoriahNV.jpg; p. 13 Library of Congress Prints and Photographs Division; pp. 15, 16 Hulton Archive/Getty Images; p. 19 © AP Images; p. 21 http://en.wikipedia.org/wiki/File:Nevada_Govenors_Mansion.JPG; p. 22 © www.istockphoto.com/Eric Renard; p. 27 http://en.wikipedia.org/wiki/File:Tahoe.JPG; p. 28 © www.istockphoto.com/Kathy Steen; p. 32 Harry How/Getty Images; p. 34 National Archives and Records Administration; p. 36 Chip Somodevilla/Getty Images; p. 39 (left) Courtesy Robesus, Inc.; p. 40 (left) http://en.wikipedia.org/wiki/File:Mountain_Bluebird.jpg; p. 40 (right) http://en.wikipedia.org/wiki/File:Sagebrushsjc.JPG.

Designer: Les Kanturek; Editor: Nick Croce
Photo Researcher: Amy Feinberg